make
yourself
COZY

Also by Katie Vaz
Don't Worry, Eat Cake

make yourself COZY

a guide for practicing self-care

KATIE VAZ

Andrews McMeel
PUBLISHING®

Andrews McMeel Publishing
a division of Andrews McMeel Universal
1130 Walnut Street, Kansas City, Missouri 64106

www.andrewsmcmeel.com

18 19 20 21 22 SDB 10 9 8 7 6 5 4 3 2 1

ISBN: 978-1-4494-9368-4

Library of Congress Control Number: 2018932803

Editor: Patty Rice
Art Director: Holly Swayne
Production Editor: Dave Shaw
Production Manager: Tamara Haus

ATTENTION: SCHOOLS AND BUSINESSES
Andrews McMeel books are available at quantity discounts with bulk purchase for educational, business, or sales promotional use. For information, please e-mail the Andrews McMeel Publishing Special Sales Department: specialsales@amuniversal.com.

to joby,
for always making
my heart feel cozy.

hello.

This book is an illustrated guide for the everyday practice of self-care. By focusing on the cozy pleasures of life, like soft blankets and the comforting scent of freshly baked bread, I believe that good feelings and contentment can be found each day. Too often "me time" is accompanied by feelings of guilt or selfishness, and it's the first item to go on a busy day's to-do list. I created this book to be a soothing guide that promotes the importance of "me time" and its necessity in self-care. With inspiration drawn from the Danish concept of "*hygge*," my hope is that this book encourages you to seek well-being through slowing down, creating an atmosphere of coziness, and taking genuine pleasure in the ordinary.

Some pages have simple tips and uncomplicated tasks to promote coziness for you to try, and others have prompts to encourage you to add your own content. Bits of heartwarming, inspirational sayings are sprinkled in there, too, for those days when our anxious minds are a best friend and a worst enemy at the same time. This guide is inspired by my own personal experiences with having anxiety and the tendency to greatly overthink everything, and by the self-care tips and prompts that I have found useful in my own life.

I hope that this book will feel like a hug to your heart and be a comforting tool in helping you slow down and find contentment through the simple act of being cozy.

SPEND A FEW MINUTES STRETCHING YOUR BODY.

Reach as far as you can!

MOVE!

Dance, run, jump, walk.

Release those emotions
that are building.

HOW ABOUT A MORNING WALK in a FOREST OR PARK with a FRIEND*?

*Furry friends are nice, too.

TODAY IS A _____ MUSIC KIND OF DAY.

Close your eyes and let yourself zone out to a few tunes today.

MIX + MATCH

 hot tea

 fresh-brewed coffee

 hot water with lemon

 hot cocoa

+

 fuzzy socks

 cloud-like pillow

 super soft blanket

 fluffy robe

 stretchy pants

+

 good book

 warm animal

 something binge-worthy

 soothing tunes

=

INSTANT COZY TOWN

add a little pretty to your home.

SWING BY A LOCAL FLORIST TODAY OR PICK A FEW WILDFLOWERS OUTSIDE.

BRING HOME SOME PLANTS TO CARE FOR.

Try these easy-to-keep-alive houseplants:

good for people
who travel often

PONYTAIL PALM
cat + dog safe

BOSTON FERN
cat + dog safe

← a cute
succulent

JADE PLANT
Not safe for pets

← improves
air quality

SNAKE PLANT
Not safe for pets

SPIDER PLANT
cat + dog safe

What in your home
feels most warm and
familiar to you?

_____

_____

What about it makes
your heart feel warm
and happy?

_____

_____

WHAT'S YOUR FAVORITE ROOM IN YOUR HOME?

A. kitchen

B. bedroom

C. office

D. dining room

E. _____

draw →

WHY IS IT YOUR FAVORITE?

_____

_____

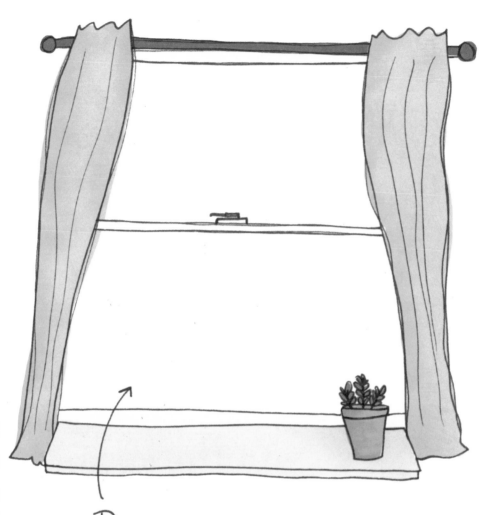

Draw what cozy weather looks like to you.

decorations
that make
you happy

cozy lighting

comfy
chair

soft
blanket
for snuggling
under

a little stool
or table for
snacks and
drinks

SET UP A COZY NOOK IN YOUR HOME.

COZY TEA TIME FOR ONE.

a chubby tea pot

your favorite mug

a simple flower or plant

cute, little, bite-sized cookies

a slice of sweet quick bread

a captivating story

YUMMY QUICK BREADS TO MAKE:

zucchini chocolate chip loaf

banana walnut bread

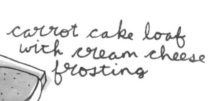

carrot cake loaf with cream cheese frosting

pumpkin spice bread

cranberry bread with an orange glaze

BE TOASTY
ON THE
INSIDE.

GO MAKE YOURSELF
SOMETHING WARM TO DRINK.

DARK CHOCOLATE
HOT COCOA

with homemade
whipped cream
and
marshmallows

HOT MULLED CIDER
with a stick of cinnamon

spicy
chai tea
latte
WITH
COCONUT MILK

MIX & MATCH

PICK A BREAKFAST

blueberry pancakes

pumpkin oatmeal

toasty bagel sandwich

PICK SOMETHING TO DO

pet animals at a local shelter

read outside

learn how to do a really cool braid

26

PICK A WAY TO UNWIND AT NIGHT

catch up on your favorite show

start a new knitting project

do some gentle yoga

=

COZY SATURDAY

mix & match
OATMEAL
recipe for one

START WITH:

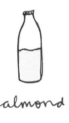 ½ cup of old-fashioned rolled oats

↓

CHOOSE A MILK:

almond   *or*   dairy   *or*   soy

↓

CHOOSE A FLAVOR:

   *or*   *or*

half a banana, sliced   ⅓ cup of berries (fresh or frozen)   2 tbsp. of canned pumpkin

ADD SOME MIX-INS:

2 tbsp. of shredded coconut

½ tsp. of chia seeds

a sprinkle of cinnamon and nutmeg to taste

¼ cup of chopped pecans or walnuts

↓

Combine ingredients in a small saucepan and cook on medium high heat for about 5 minutes, stirring frequently to prevent oatmeal from sticking to the bottom. Once oatmeal begins to bubble, let it cook for another 2-3 minutes, stirring frequently. Cover with a tight-fitting lid and remove from heat. Let sit for about 10 minutes, or until most of the liquid has absorbed. Serve warm.

↓

ADD SOME TOPPINGS:

a drizzle of maple syrup

1 tbsp. of pepitas

1 tbsp. of nut butter

a dollop of cream cheese

1 tbsp. of jam

SPICES
TO GIVE YOU
THE WARM FUZZIES

CINNAMON

FAVORITE USES:

- sprinkle on toast with honey
- sprinkle with sugar on apple slices for a cozy snack

NUTMEG

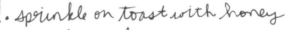

FAVORITE USES:

- sprinkle a little on your morning coffee
- add a pinch or two to your favorite snickerdoodle recipe

CURRY POWDER

FAVORITE USES:
- add to veggie soups to create warmth
- sprinkle on butternut squash or sweet potatoes before roasting

CLOVES

FAVORITE USES:
- mix a small pinch into pumpkin oatmeal
- a classic for spicy gingerbread treats

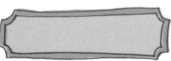

FAVORITE USES:

← What is another spice that seems cozy to you?

LAVENDER

EARL GREY

GREEN TEA

cranberry orange

Host a small
tea and scone
party for a few friends.

blueberry buttermilk

DARJEELING

pumpkin walnut

CHAMOMILE

lemon poppyseed

PICK OUT AND LEARN HOW TO MAKE A NEW NOURISHING RECIPE

from scratch.

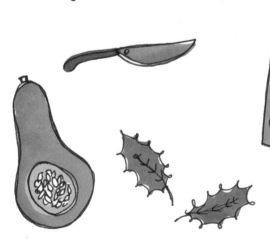

MIX & MATCH

CHOOSE A BLANKET

flannel

fleece

knitted

CHOOSE A SNACK

good cheese

warm dessert

toast with your favorite topping

CHOOSE SOME COMPANY

phone call with a loved one

peace and quiet

a podcast

=

COMFY COUCH TIME

Anatomy of a simple CHEESE PLATTER

some sweets

a creamy cheese

Cheddar

a sharp cheese

brie

a little something salty and savory

goat cheese

a fresh cheese

some crunchy stuff

try this simple spread to make a weekday evening feel more special. even if it's just for you.

WHICH TEXTURES FEEL MOST SNUGGLY TO YOU?

wool

silk

velvet

fleece

← draw more

SPEND A FEW MINUTES TODAY massaging your hands WITH A LOVELY SCENTED LOTION.

jasmine
lotion

which scents are soothing to you?

cinnamon

lavender

clean laundry

fresh, warm bread

bright citrus

↑ draw more

draw more →

A GOOD BELLY LAUGH IS VITAL EVERY NOW AND THEN.

Describe the last time you laughed so hard it hurt (in a good way):

_____

_____

_____

_____

_____

_____

_____

_____

_____

_____

PICK A RAINY DAY ACTIVITY

Follow a DIY tutorial to craft something charming for your home

Cook up something wholesome from scratch for you or your family

Dive into a subject that really interests you with books or documentaries. Let your curiosity guide you!

Draw something else you might enjoy

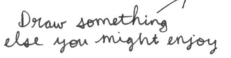

START A CLUB WITH SOME FRIENDS.

Meet regularly and enjoy being in the company of others who share your interests.

birding

quilting

French cooking

PICK OUT A DOUGH RECIPE THAT REQUIRES AT LEAST A WHOLE DAY TO CREATE.

Block off some time and let yourself become absorbed in the process and sensory experience of baking.

ESCAPE INTO YOUR FAVORITE BOOK.

Why is it your favorite?

TRUTH
CONNECTION
TENDERNESS
Serenity
COURAGE
amusement
WONDER
Enchantment
ADVENTURE

What's your favorite part?
What do you feel when you read it?

CHOOSE A LOCATION TO READ OUTSIDE

your
porch

local
park

outdoor
cafe

draw another
outdoor space you'd
like to read in

CREATE A HANDMADE CARD FOR A FRIEND *and* MAIL IT TO THEM.

YOU ARE SUCH A WONDERFUL & KIND HUMAN

(even if they live in the same town as you).

Decorate a cake with the prettiest sprinkles you can find.

A WARM DRINK
and a
CHANGE OF SCENERY
MIGHT BE NICE.

Where can you go to change things up?

on a walk

to a coffee shop

to a friend's house

where else could you go?

COZY FOOD UPGRADE

Grilled Cheese Sandwich

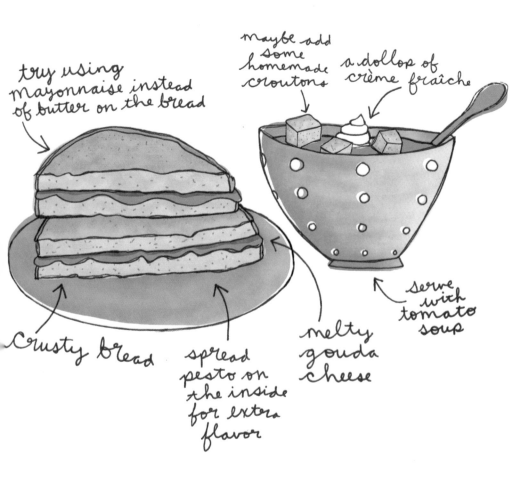

try using mayonnaise instead of butter on the bread

maybe add some homemade croutons

a dollop of crème fraîche

Crusty bread

spread pesto on the inside for extra flavor

melty gouda cheese

serve with tomato soup

···Mix & Match···

pizza with
homemade dough

a classic
roast

creamy
baked pasta

a fragrant, simmering
soup with crusty bread

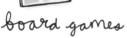

board games

watch party

craft night

dining room

living room

garden patio

A COZY DINNER PARTY

MAKE IT GLOW.

Create warmth
with gentle lighting.

HOST A SMALL GAME NIGHT WITH A FEW FRIENDS.

Play some board games while something tasty simmers on your stove.

IT'S OKAY TO TREAT YOURSELF TO SOME UNABASHED GUILTY PLEASURE TV SHOW OR MOVIE SOMETIMES.

HAVE BREAKFAST FOR DINNER.

Comfy, stretchy clothes and slippers are encouraged.

IF ALL BUSINESSES WERE ALWAYS CLOSED ON SUNDAYS. HOW WOULD YOU SPEND THAT DAY?

get outside

savor home-cooked meals

_____

_____

_____

_____

_____

_____

unplug

rest

Treat yourself to Sundays like this when you can sometimes.

start a new hobby

catch up with loved ones

On dark winter mornings, allow some extra time to wake up slowly while having breakfast by candlelight.

COOK or BAKE SOMETHING FOR A FRIEND WHO COULD USE SOME CHEERING UP.

It's a simple gesture that might mean the world to someone. It might even help distract you from your worries.

something nostalgic and comforting

something hearty and nourishing

something doughy and sweet

What else could you make?

HOMEMADE JAM CAN BE A LOVELY GIFT FOR A FRIEND (OR YOURSELF).

Berry Chia Jam

YOU'LL NEED:

- 2 cups fresh berries
- 2 tbsp. real maple syrup
- 1 tbsp. lemon juice
- 2 tbsp. chia seeds

1. Prepare the fruit. Remove stems and pits, if any. Hull and chop strawberries. Small berries can be left whole.

2. In a medium saucepan, combine the berries, maple syrup, and lemon juice. Cook over medium high heat for 5-10 minutes, stirring frequently, until saucy. Mash the berries lightly a bit with a fork.

3. Stir in the chia seeds and reduce the heat to medium low. Cook for another 15-20 minutes, stirring frequently until the sauce thickens.

4. Remove from heat. Once the jam has cooled to room temperature, transfer to a jar. Your chia jam can be stored in the fridge for up to one week.

Spoon onto oatmeal, yogurt, toast, ice cream.

HAVE A COZY

where will you sleep?

HOME

A TENT

A LOCAL BED & BREAKFAST

who will be your company?

YOUR FURRY FRIEND

YOUR BFF

YOUR FAMILY

STAYCATION

where will you eat?

A FOOD TRUCK

A BAKERY

A DINER

what will you do?

HAVE A PICNIC

SIGN UP FOR A CRAFTING CLASS

VISIT AN UNUSUAL MUSEUM

MIX & MATCH

roomy cardigan

snuggly hoodie

fuzzy scarf

knitted beanie

+

flowy dress

wooly sweater

soft cotton t-shirt

flannel button-up

+

black tights

favorite jeans

stretchy yoga pants

+

warm boots

cushy flats

comfy sneakers

=

A COZY OUTFIT

DRESSES & TIGHTS

(possibly the coziest outfit ever!)

outfit keeps looking cuter with each layer added (like scarves, sweaters, jackets)

perfect for mild or chilly weather (the "in-between seasons")

black tights go with everything, but quirky patterns or colors are fun, too!

bonus if the dress has pockets

stretchy and soft (feels pretty much just like wearing pajamas)

toasty, warm socks

pairs well with comfy boots

WOULD YOU RATHER...

☐ read your favorite book   **OR**   ☐ watch your favorite movie

☐ nap in a hammock   **OR**   ☐ nap in a beach chair

☐ bake a lasagna   **OR**   ☐ bake a cake

☐ warm up by a fireplace   **OR**   ☐ warm up by a campfire

☐ wear a flannel shirt   **OR**   ☐ sleep in flannel sheets

SURROUND YOURSELF WITH THE EXQUISITE AROMA OF OLD BOOKS.

Visit your neighborhood library and check out a few books.

TODAY IS THE SPECIAL OCCASION

Pull out all those special things you save and use them today.

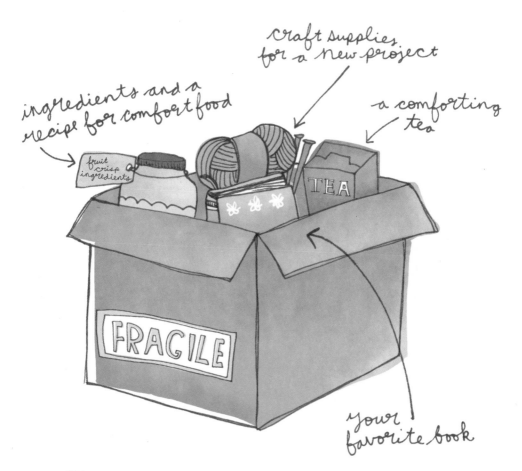

ingredients and a recipe for comfort food

fruit crisp ingredients

craft supplies for a new project

a comforting tea

TEA

FRAGILE

your favorite book

CREATE A COZY CARE PACKAGE TO GIVE TO A FRIEND.

Fill it with heartwarming things that cheer you up.

FRUIT CRISP
RECIPE

YOU'LL NEED:

½ cup + 2 tbsp. all-purpose flour

½ cup whole-wheat flour

½ cup old-fashioned rolled oats

½ cup packed brown sugar

½ tsp. ground cinnamon

⅛ tsp. ground nutmeg

¼ tsp. salt

½ cup butter, melted

3 tbsp. white sugar

1 tbsp. lemon juice

CHOOSE YOUR FRUIT:

    OR

about 6 medium/large apples, peeled, cored, sliced

4 cups fresh berries, stems removed (if any)

You can experiment with your own favorite combinations of fruit, too!

Preheat oven to 350°F.

In a large bowl, stir together the fruit, white sugar, and lemon juice. Sprinkle 2 tbsp. of all-purpose flour over the fruit and gently stir. Set aside.

For the topping, stir together the rest of the all-purpose flour, whole-wheat flour, oats, brown sugar, cinnamon, nutmeg, and salt in another bowl. Pour in the melted butter and stir to incorporate.

Grease a baking dish or pie plate that is about 9" in diameter. Pour in the fruit mixture, then spoon clumps of the topping evenly over the fruit.

Bake for 50-60 minutes or until topping is golden brown and fruit is bubbly.

Serve warm and be cozy.

SPEND A FEW MINUTES IN THE
SUNSHINE TODAY. DRINK AN EXTRA
GLASS OF WATER.

OCCASIONALLY, PRETEND LIKE IT'S LAST CENTURY AND SOCIAL MEDIA ISN'T A THING.

THIS OR THAT

WHICH FEELS COZIER TO YOU?

  FALL

- ☐ pumpkin pie **OR** ☐ apple pie
- ☐ carved pumpkins **OR** ☐ painted pumpkins
- ☐ knitted scarf **OR** ☐ flannel scarf
- ☐ chai flavor **OR** ☐ pumpkin spice flavor
- ☐ crisp, cold cider **OR** ☐ toasty, hot cider
- ☐ a train ride to see foliage **OR** ☐ a road trip to see foliage

WINTER

- [ ] sugar cookies **OR** [ ] gingerbread cookies
- [ ] building a snowman **OR** [ ] making a snow angel
- [ ] peppermint mocha latte **OR** [ ] eggnog latte
- [ ] rustic holiday decor **OR** [ ] retro holiday decor
- [ ] wool mittens **OR** [ ] fleece gloves
- [ ] ice skating **OR** [ ] snowshoeing

a warm blanket

an intriguing story

a crackling fire

percolated coffee

Welcome

GO CAMPING IN THE FALL.

Breathe in crisp, fresh air and snack on s'mores.

cinnamon graham crackers

gooey fire-roasted marshmallow

chocolate hazelnut spread

COZY CAMPFIRE
S'MORES

toasted or charred? which is your favorite?

FESTIVE FALL TIP

Next time you carve pumpkins, try sprinkling cinnamon on the bottom side of the cut-out top.

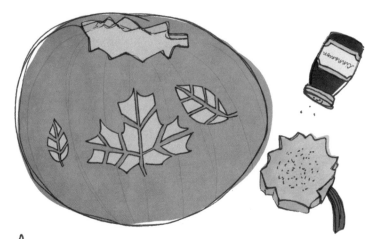

When you light the pumpkin with a candle, the warmth will create a delicious scent that smells like pie.

WE ARE ALL IN THIS TOGETHER

GO STARGAZING ONCE IN A WHILE.

What do you feel when you ponder the universe?

_____

_____

_____

_____

CREATE A BUCKET LIST
FOR EACH SEASON.

Write down some activities that you'll look forward to doing each season.

FALL

things to do:

_____ _____

_____ _____

places to go:

_____ _____

_____ _____

things to eat:

_____

_____

_____

_____

WINTER

things to do:

_____ _____

_____ _____

places to go:

_____ _____

_____ _____

things to eat:

_____

_____

_____

_____

SPRING

things to do:

_____ _____

_____ _____

places to go:

_____ _____

_____ _____

things
to eat:

_____

_____

_____

_____

SUMMER

things to do:

_____ _____

_____ _____

places to go:

_____ _____

_____ _____

things
to eat:

_____

_____

_____

_____

fill these CLOUDS

with words that make you feel light and free.

BREAK UP A MONOTONOUS WEEKDAY.

Pack your lunch and eat al fresco. Visualize the fresh air and nutrition recharging your body.

WRAP YOURSELF in an OVERSIZED CARDIGAN and MAKE A CUP OF WARM, SPICY TEA TO LIVEN up a DREARY, GRAY DAY.

recipe for a
Heart Hug

INGREDIENTS:

- a sprinkle of support via a BFF phone call
- a cup of something warm and toasty to drink
- a dash of fresh air
- one oversized, super soft sweater to burrow in
- a smidgen of dark chocolate

DIRECTIONS:

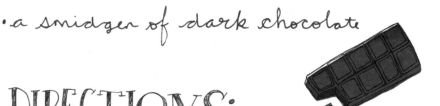

Combine all ingredients when needed. Recipe can easily be doubled. Coziness may last a couple of days.

Sometimes something simple like sparkly glitter and glue can help cheer up a crummy day.

Here are a few ideas for easy glitter projects.

decoupage glitter inside an old jar

make a photograph seem extra joyful

decorate a plant pot

create a happy string of bunting

have any other ideas in mind?

PAINT YOUR NAILS IN A FEEL-GOOD COLOR.

Add polka dots, stripes, or glitter if you are feeling creative.

BE YOUR OWN FRIEND.

If loved ones were going through this, what would you say to them?

_____

_____

_____

_____

_____

_____

_____

_____

_____

_____

FIND A PRETTY NOTEBOOK and fill it with COMPLIMENTS YOU RECEIVE, NO MATTER HOW SMALL.

LITTLE BOOK OF COMPLIMENTS

nice
things
nice
people
have
said
to
me.

Refer back to it
as needed.

TAKE YOURSELF on a DATE.

Wear something that makes you feel lovely. Treat yourself to something delicious.

IS THERE A HOBBY YOU'VE BEEN CURIOUS TO TRY?

Mark it in your calendar and set aside guilt-free time weekly.

ink

sketch book

calligraphy set

learn how to speak NORWEGIAN

HUNT FOR SOMETHING CHARMING at a LOCAL THRIFT SHOP.

Did you find something to wear? To look at? To use? To be comfy in?

Fill in this pie chart
with how much of your
free time is spent doing
the following.

HOW I USE MY FREE TIME

▥ worrying about
the future

▨ overthinking
situations

▩ comparing
myself to
others

▤ fixating on
past mistakes

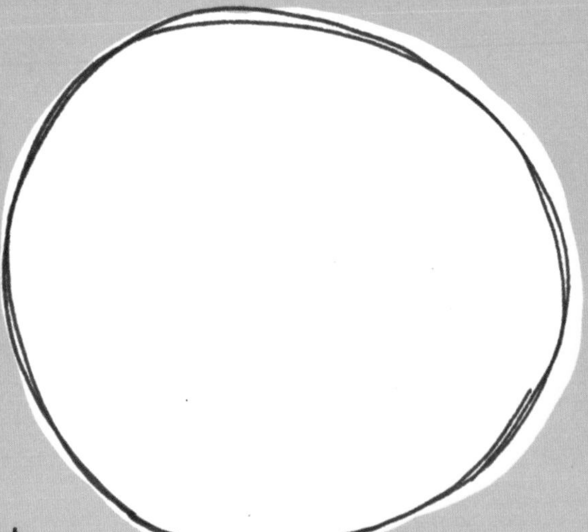

Now, pick four activities
that make you happy
to replace each category
in the new pie chart below.

HOW I ⋚COULD⋚ USE MY FREE TIME

▯▯▯ _____

▦ _____

▨ _____

≋ _____

MAKE A DATE TO GO FOR A WALK WITH A FRIEND REGULARLY.

Enjoy each other's company, whether that is a comfortable silence or time spent chatting about similar interests.

WHICH IS YOUR FAVORITE SEASON TO GO FOR WALKS?

FALL

WINTER

SPRING

SUMMER

TAKE THE EDGE OFF A ROUGH DAY BY UNWINDING IN A WARM BATH OR SHOWER.

Pay attention to the soothing feeling of warm water on your skin.

hello, pretty

Pick something soft to wrap yourself in.

soft cotton robe

flannel blanket

knitted scarf

fluffy comforter

fleece-lined sweatshirt

Treat yourself to the
fluffiest of socks.

Make tonight

EXTRA SNUGGLY.

WASH ALL OF YOUR SHEETS AND MAKE YOUR BED.

MIX & MATCH

activity to unwind

put on
a face
mask

write in
a journal

take a warm
shower

read a
novel

+

night attire

flannel
pajamas

flowy
nightgown

silky set

t-shirt
and
shorts

calming scents

some lavender
pillow spray

rich, velvety
lotion

your
favorite
candle

fragrant
herbal tea

+

soothing sounds

the
outdoors

a fan

tranquil
music

an audio
book

=

CALM, COZY
NIGHTTIME UNWIND

glowing string lights

some art that speaks to you

comfy pajamas to sleep in

a few squishy pillows

a photo that warms your heart

a pretty plant

a soft fitted sheet

a warm companion

a fluffy, oversized duvet

a lineup of books you look forward to reading

an extra fuzzy throw

a soft rug for chilly mornings

ANATOMY OF A COZY BEDROOM

THINK OF WHO MAKES YOUR SOUL HAPPIEST.

Write their names and draw their faces below.

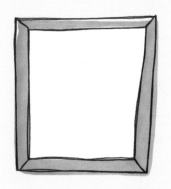

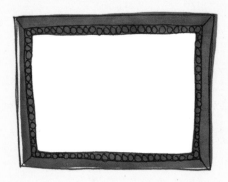

Wouldn't it be SO FREEING...

* to not be afraid of _____?

* if I worried less about _____?

* if I remembered more often that I'm really good at _____?

* if I could forgive myself for _____?

* if I _____ more often?

* if I felt more proud of myself when _____?

* if I could always remember that _____ is most important?

ALL PROGRESS COUNTS.

even the tiniest bits.

a cosy
FIRST AID
KIT

remedies
for tender hearts

Fill in with remedies that work for you.

this food
warms my
belly and
my heart

↑ this book
always fills me
with comfort

a chat with this person who always knows just what to say

_____

this movie/TV show always makes me laugh and feel light

_____

this type of exercise makes me feel alive and healthy

_____

Refer back to this "kit" on rough days and use as needed.

CLOSE YOUR EYES
AND FOCUS ON THE
SOUNDS AROUND YOU.

What do you hear?

_____

What is the farthest
sound you can hear?

_____

This can help distract you
when you feel anxiety creeping in.

GIVE YOURSELF A TIME LIMIT FOR WHAT IS BOTHERING YOU.

Set a date in the future for when you'll allow yourself to revisit the options you are considering. You might feel entirely different by then.

Meanwhile, try to be okay with not having an answer or solution yet.

THINK OF YOUR "ME TIME" AS A FRIEND.

Stick up for her when needed and hang out often.

TRUE OR FALSE?

T   F

☐ ☐ What you need is sometimes different from what others need.

☐ ☐ You've survived some pretty tough things.

☐ ☐ Your heart is capable of loving fiercely.

☐ ☐ Worrying generally solves nothing.

☐ ☐ Being human means being imperfect.

THINK ABOUT ALL THE THINGS YOU'VE BEEN THROUGH IN YOUR LIFE. WRITE DOWN A FEW THAT WERE PARTICULARLY DIFFICULT.

a. _____

b. _____

c. _____

d. _____

NOW, ADD THESE EXPERIENCES TO THE ACHIEVEMENTS ON THE OTHER PAGE.

Dealt with _____ in a mature way!

Experienced _____ and am still a good human.

Survived _____

Was able to find bits of happiness in the world, even after _____

Sometimes we are doing better in life than we think.

IS THERE A SITUATION THAT PARTICULARLY WORRIES YOU?

Write down some outcomes that you fear will happen, then write down how you might be able to handle each one.

WORRISOME OUTCOME:

_____

WHAT ARE SOME STEPS YOU COULD TAKE TO WORK THROUGH THIS?

_____

_____

_____

WHO COULD HELP YOU AND WHAT MIGHT THEY SAY TO COMFORT YOU?

_____

_____

_____

WORRISOME OUTCOME:

WHAT ARE SOME STEPS YOU COULD TAKE TO WORK THROUGH THIS?

WHO COULD HELP YOU AND WHAT MIGHT THEY SAY TO COMFORT YOU?

Maybe the worst-case scenarios seem less scary when you have a game plan.

NOTICE SENSATIONS WHEN YOU START TO FEEL UNGROUNDED.

What do you hear?
What do you smell?
What do your hands
and feet feel?

melancholy

worry

panic

fear

TRY TO OBSERVE YOUR FEELINGS WITHOUT JUDGMENT.

Watch them come and go.
See how they drift by like clouds.

You are not defined by them.

SELF-CARE ISN'T SELFISH AND IT DOESN'T HAVE TO REQUIRE MUCH TIME.

Can you take just 10 minutes here or there to squeeze in some me time? Sip something warm and cozy. Read a few pages from a novel you like, savor some fresh air.

What else could you do that might only take 10 minutes or so?

_____   _____

_____   _____

_____   _____

IT IS OKAY TO BE UNCOMFORTABLE SOMETIMES.

The feeling is temporary, and eventually it will pass. Until then, make yourself cozy.

thank you

To Patty Rice, my editor, and everyone at Andrews McMeel Publishing for all of your kind encouragement and for helping me bring my dream projects alive. To my agent, Laurie Abkemeier, for your invaluable support and guidance—I'm incredibly grateful for the day you discovered my work. To my lovely friends near and far, who are always there to comfort, congratulate, and listen. To my mom, Pat Vaz, and my sister, Sarah Vaz, for unconditionally cheering me on and nurturing every hope and dream of mine. And finally, to my husband and best friend, Joby Springsteen, for your unwavering faith in me. I'm so happy I get to do life with you.

about the author

KATIE VAZ is an illustrator, author, hand-letterer, and graphic designer. She also designs her own line of greeting cards, prints, and other stationery products, which are sold both online and in brick and mortar shops across North America. Her cards capture the sticky sweet, awkward but funny, sometimes emotionally heavy things that need to be said in all types of relationships. Katie is the author of the adult coloring book *Don't Worry, Eat Cake*. Katie also works as a freelance illustrator and designer on a variety of branding, illustration, print, and packaging projects. Her work has been featured on Buzzfeed.com, RealSimple.com, WomansDay.com, POPSUGAR.com, and in *Time Out New York* magazine. She studied graphic design (BFA) at the Rochester Institute of Technology in Rochester, New York, and integrated design (MA) at Anhalt University of Applied Sciences in Dessau, Germany. Katie likes to spend her free time baking, playing with cats, and traveling the world. She lives in Upstate New York and online at www.katievaz.com.